SEVILLE
THE CITY AT A GLANCE

Torre Triana
Francisco Javier Sáenz de Oiza's vast, circular 55m-high government office sits seemingly on its own, looming menacingly over the river.
See p077

Torre Panorámica Schindler
Built for Expo 92, this 65m steel elevator now forms part of Pabellón de la Navegación, in the city where Christopher Columbus is buried. Cesar Pelli's nearby Torre Cajasol is set to rise above it by 100m or so.
See p072

Antiguo Mercado del Barranco
The 1883 fishmarket serves as an exhib. hall. A gourmet food market is planned.
Calle Arjona 28

Puente de la Barqueta
Featuring a steel arch spanning 214m, and triangular porticoes at either end, this bridge is unmissable when lit up at night.

La Maestranza
After Las Ventas in Madrid, Seville's 1761 La Maestranza (The Armoury) is considered the best bullfighting arena in the country.
See p014

Teatro de la Maestranza
A 1,800-seat theatre that attracts the glitterati to opera performances and concerts by the renowned Real Orquesta Sinfónica de Sevilla.
Paseo de Cristóbal Colón 22

La Giralda
Once the minaret of the mosque when the city was Moorish, and now the cathedral belltower, La Giralda has been the visual focal point of the old town for more than 800 years.
See p013

INTRODUCTION
THE CHANGING FACE OF THE URBAN SCENE

Seville is an easy sell. It entices three-and-a-half-million visitors a year with its seductive imagery. The sultry, fan-waving señoritas, bullfighters dressed in gold and silk, gypsy flamenco dancers and seemingly endless afternoons – Spain's fourth-largest city enjoys more sunshine than any other major destination in Europe. It's no accident, then, that the Andalusian capital has inspired two of the most sexually provocative characters in fiction: tragic femme fatale Carmen, who rolled cigars on her thighs while concealing a knife in her garter belt, and the dashing lothario Don Juan, who set off from here to conquer the hearts of women around the world.

Since it hosted Expo 92 – a vital catalyst that brought good contemporary architecture and a cosmopolitan edge to this deeply traditional place – Seville developed considerably. And although the economic crisis has slowed progress, it has not stopped it, with the bonus of making the city more affordable. An ambitious urban regeneration project (see p044) breathed life into the city centre, and a raft of chic boutique hotels and dynamic restaurants have opened in the past few years. A sharp influx of foreign residents and students has helped to integrate Seville's heritage with global influences, giving rise to sushi tapas, flamenco rappers and slick hammam-style spas. Here, we steer clear of the tourist snares and explore the modern face of southern Spain's vibrant heart, without excluding the history and ceremony that make it unmissable.

ESSENTIAL INFO
FACTS, FIGURES AND USEFUL ADDRESSES

TOURIST OFFICE
Plaza del Triunfo 1
T 954 210 005
www.turismosevilla.org

TRANSPORT
Airport transfer to city centre
www.tussam.es
Buses depart every 25 minutes, from 5am to 12.30am. The journey takes 30 minutes
Car hire
Hertz
T 954 538 331
Metro
www.metro-sevilla.es
Trains run Monday to Thursday, 6am to 11pm; Friday, 6.30am to 2am; Saturday, 7.30am to 2am; Sunday, 7.30am to 11pm
Taxis
Radio Taxi
T 954 580 000

EMERGENCY SERVICES
Emergencies
T 112
24-hour pharmacy
Farmacia Concepción de los Reyes
Calle Amador de los Ríos 33
T 954 421 153

CONSULATES
British Consulate
Edificio Eurocom
Calle Mauricio Moro Pareto 2
Malaga
T 902 109 356
www.ukinspain.fco.gov.uk
US Consulate
Second floor
Plaza Nueva 8-8 duplicado
T 954 218 751
madrid.usembassy.gov

POSTAL SERVICES
Post office
Avenida de la Constitución 2
T 954 224 760
Shipping
Mail Boxes Etc
Calle Jesús del Gran Poder 45
T 954 915 519

BOOKS
British Pavilion, Seville Exposition 1992: Nicholas Grimshaw and Partners
by Colin Davies (Phaidon Press)
Seville, Córdoba and Granada: A Cultural and Literary History
by Elizabeth Nash (Signal Books)

WEBSITES
Art/Culture
www.caac.es
www.icas-sevilla.org
Newspaper
www.abcdesevilla.es

EVENTS
La Bienal de Flamenco
www.labienal.com
Feria de Abril
feriadesevilla.andalunet.com

COST OF LIVING
Taxi from San Pablo Airport to city centre
€25
Cappuccino
€1.50
Packet of cigarettes
€4.50
Daily newspaper
€1.35
Bottle of champagne
€80

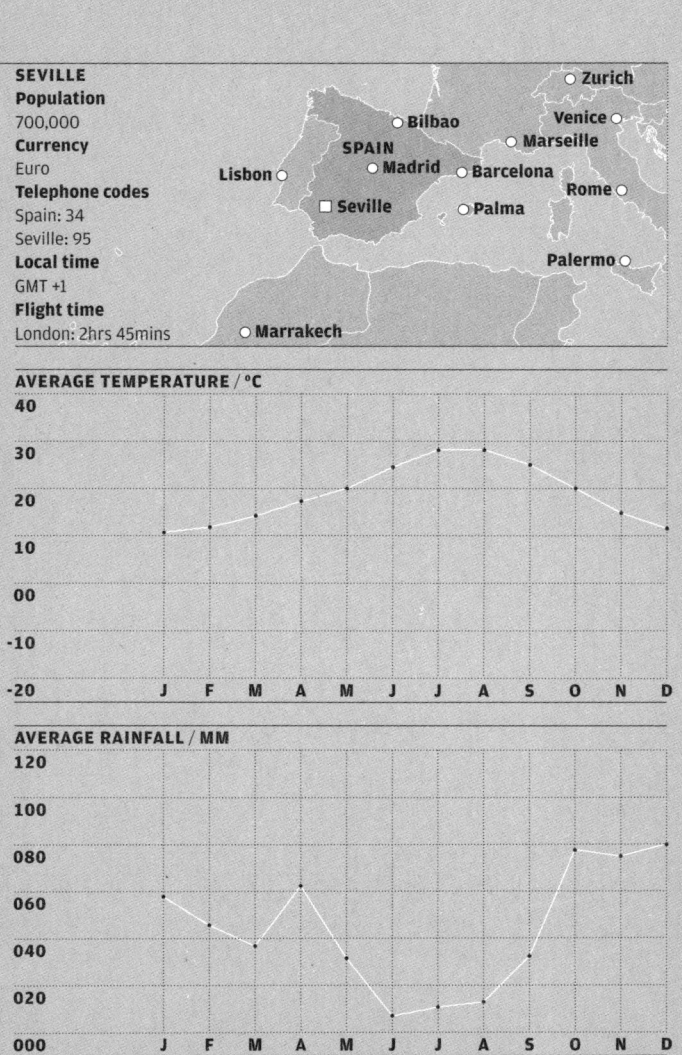

NEIGHBOURHOODS
THE AREAS YOU NEED TO KNOW AND WHY

To help you navigate the city, we've chosen the most interesting districts (see below and the map inside the back cover) and colour-coded our featured venues, according to their location; those venues that are outside these areas are not coloured.

LA MACARENA
Decades of restoration have moved this deeply religious, working-class barrio up in the world. Head here for flamenco bars and tapas dives, such as El Rinconcillo (Calle Gerona 40, T 954 223 183). The nuns of the 15th-century Monasterio de Santa Paula (Calle Santa Paula 11, T 954 536 330) sell *mermelada* from their orange groves.

LOS REMEDIOS
This residential neighbourhood is home to many of the city's main sports complexes, including Club Náutico (Avenida de Sanlúcar de Barrameda, T 954 454 777), a smart sailing/rowing venue. The world's largest flamenco festival, the Feria de Abril, is held here, drawing more than a million visitors.

LA CARTUJA
Several buildings, such as the svelte curve of Pabellón de Finlandia (see p073), still stand on this Expo 92 site, in the north of the city. Other reasons to visit are the Centro Andaluz de Arte Contemporáneo (see p039), and some of Seville's best clubs, notably Antique Theatro (see p066).

EL ARENAL
La Maestranza bullring (see p014) is the focal point of this tourist hub. There are plenty of classic Andalusian restaurants, and venues such as Hijos de E Morales (see p070) where you can order sherry from oak casks. The bars and terraces along the river are ideal for beating the summer heat.

MARÍA LUISA
At the heart of the city's largest green space, Parque de María Luisa (see p088), are the manicured gardens and pavilions built for the 1929 Ibero-American Expo, and the grand folly of Plaza de España, the setting for many Hollywood epics. Also look out for El Costurero de la Reina, a fine example of neo-Mudejar architecture.

TRIANA
A lure for tapas lovers, thanks to earthy venues such as Sol y Sombra (see p056), Triana boasts many nightspots along Calle del Betis, from discos to live music and flamenco venues, including El Rejoneo (No 31) and Lo Nuestro (No 33). Cross the river via the elegant 19th-century Puente Triana.

SAN VICENTE
Seville's creatives have decamped to hip Alameda de Hércules (see p012). Artists, musicians and students flock to its bars, cafés, such as República (see p058), and restaurants like the bijou Eslava (see p046). The old-school still exists in the rough and ready Casa Paco (No 23, T 954 900 148).

SANTA CRUZ
Stylish hotel conversions, like Palacio de Villapanés (see p017), and posh residences pepper the old Jewish quarter, a maze of medieval streets lined with whitewashed houses, flower-filled patios and quirky bars such as La Fresquita (Calle Mateos Gago 29, T 954 226 010), filled with Catholic icons.

LANDMARKS
THE SHAPE OF THE CITY SKYLINE

Seville is expanding fast, thanks largely to bold initiatives by its civic leaders. Keen to propel the city into the 21st century, they have secured such adventurous interventions as the Metropol Parasol (see p044), a futuristic, mushroom-shaped market canopy, and Seville's first skyscraper, the elliptic Torre Cajasol, designed by Pelli Clarke Pelli and slated for 2013. On the site of the 1992 Expo, its 37 floors will be topped by a public terrace and restaurant.

Historic landmarks include some superb examples of the local baroque style, including the Palacio de San Telmo (Avenida de Roma, T 955 035 500), located near the Real Fábrica de Tabacos (Calle San Fernando, T 954 551 000), which provided the original setting for Bizet's *Carmen* and is now part of the university. Further along Canal de Alfonso XIII are La Maestranza bullring (see p014), surrounded by statues of *toreros* and *toreras* (female bullfighters), the octagonal Torre del Oro (Paseo de Cristóbal Colón, T 954 222 419) and, set on the promenade, the Monumento a la Tolerancia (see p040), a concrete sculpture unmistakably by Eduardo Chillida.

Seville's most iconic structure remains its cathedral – a Gothic marvel which is the world's largest church in terms of volume. Built on the site of a pre-existing Almohad mosque, it's crowned by La Giralda (see p013), a 12th-century minaret extended to include a belfry in 1568. The views from here are the finest in the city.

For full addresses, see Resources.

010

Puente del Alamillo
When Seville was chosen to host Expo 92, a large, mainly deserted area, La Cartuja, between the canal and the Guadalquivir River, was chosen as the site where the numerous pavilions were built. Access was a priority, and by 1992 four new bridges had been constructed, the largest of which, Puente del Alamillo, was designed by Santiago Calatrava. The harp-like structure is visible from the old town, and is a spectacular sight at night. A 200m-long concrete-and-steel crossing, it has a 142m-high mast, which leans at a 58-degree angle and supports the deck with cables. Calatrava's original plan was for another, symmetrical bridge on the other side of La Cartuja, but this was never realised. Alamillo echoes the shape of the architect's Turtle Bay Sundial Bridge in Redding, California, and his Chords Bridge in Jerusalem.

Alameda de Hércules

In 1574, the Count of Barajas drained a swamp to create a public space marked by columns at each end and lined with shady poplar trees (*álamos*) that gave the square its name. Fashionable in the 17th century, La Alameda subsequently fell into decline to become Seville's red-light district. Its fortunes began to look up again in the 1990s, when it was pegged as one of the city's up-and-coming areas.

In 2009, a redesign, conceived by Spanish architects José Antonio Martínez Lapeña & Elías Torres, responsible for successful urban planning schemes in Barcelona and Toledo, among other places, was unveiled. Alameda de Hércules now has distinctive ceramic-tile paving, and a buzzing strip of eateries and terraces, pulling a crowd much less straight-laced than you will find in neighbouring Santa Cruz.

La Giralda

A former minaret, the lower two-thirds of La Giralda is all that remains of Seville's Almohad mosque. Designed by Ahmad Ibn Baso and completed in 1198, it is a close cousin of Koutoubia in Marrakech and the Hassan Tower in Rabat, and was built using ashlars – large rectangular blocks of hand-sculpted stone – some of which were sequestered from Roman remains. The belfry is a 16th-century addition, designed by Cordoba architect Hernán Ruiz, which increased the tower's height to roughly 100m. As a result of its mixed and sometimes bloody history, La Giralda is seen as an architectural totem pole of Spanish history, encompassing Roman, Moorish and the greatest expressions of the country's Gothic and baroque styles.
Avenida de la Constitución, T 902 099 692, www.catedraldesevilla.es

La Maestranza

Named after the order of knights to which it still belongs, La Maestranza hosted its first bullfight in 1761, making it the oldest major bullring in Spain. Its open, tiered stands are topped by an elegant circular colonnade that provides shade for VIPs, and, following a 2010 refurbishment, the arena holds 11,500 spectators. The royal box is tucked under handsome baroque arches bordered with azulejo-style tiles designed by Portuguese sculptor Cayetano de Acosta. Triumphant *toreros* leave through the Puerta del Principe, whereas the less fortunate end up in the surgery-quality infirmary, next door to a museum displaying costumes and portraits, and the heads of bulls, some of which earned their place by killing a matador.
Paseo de Cristóbal Colón 12, T 954 224 577, www.realmaestranza.com

HOTELS
WHERE TO STAY AND WHICH ROOMS TO BOOK

What was once a mediocre accommodation scene has become much slicker in recent years, in terms of contemporary design and quality versus price. The choice is extensive, from hip but inexpensive hostels and €30-a-night *residenciales* to three- to four-star hotels that are hard to distinguish from one another. The hot tickets are Seville's sumptuous grande dame, the Alfonso XIII (see p024), and the superbly located modern EME (see p027), which has a fine spa (see p091) and a striking arabesque patio designed by architect Juan Pedro Donaire. For more traditional Moorish surrounds, head to the low-key gem, Alcoba del Rey (see p021).

For its rooftop pool, which looks on to La Giralda (see p013), check into Hotel Doña María (see p054). In the same quarter, not far from Plaza Alfalfa, is the plush Corral del Rey (see p030) and historic Las Casas de la Judería (see p022). One tier below these, in terms of luxury and style if not service and reliability, is Hotel Adriano (Calle de Adriano 12, T 954 293 800), beside the bullring (see p014), and Sacristía de Santa Ana (Alameda de Hércules 22, T 954 915 722), a rustic and laidback boutique in an 18th-century vestry: first-floor rooms overlook the boho and ever-lively square (see p012). For groups, Almansa 11 (see p020) is a great option.

Bear in mind that Seville gets crammed with tourists in summer and during the Feria de Abril, so booking well ahead is a must. *For full addresses and room rates, see Resources.*

Palacio de Villapanés

This conversion of an 18th-century palace into a 50-room boutique hotel retained the original structural features such as the imperious facade and interior courtyards with their marble columns and porticoes (overleaf) – there's also a turret with vistas over the finest skyline in old Spain. Catalan interior designers GCA decorated the rooms in a muted palette and many, such as the Palacio Suite (above), have wood floors, painted panelled walls, high beamed ceilings and splashes of colour in the electric-blue and black mosaic tiling. Our favourite key is the Torreón suite, a 60 sq m former dovecote under the cupola with a private terrace. There's also a stylish spa and a restaurant serving contemporary Andalusian cuisine.
Calle Santiago 31, T 954 502 063,
www.almasevilla.com

Palacio de Villapanés

Almansa 11

In the heart of El Arenal, this 1910 building was designed by Aníbal González Álvarez-Ossorio, the architect of Seville's overblown Plaza de España (see p072) and numerous civic buildings. On inheriting the crumbling property in 2011, Joaquín Haro y Fernández de Córdoba restored and divided it into 17 apartments for let, from bijou studios to spacious duplexes (No 5, above) and large suites, with original carved woodwork and colourful tiling. Some come with balconies but all have high ceilings, plenty of natural light and the use of a roof terrace. The vibe is of a community of international visitors living alongside local artists and writers. There's no room service, but there are fully operational kitchens, and department store El Corte Inglés is round the corner.
Calle Almansa 11-13, T 670 343 343, www.almansa11.com

Alcoba del Rey

Located in La Macarena, next to the basilica, the Alcoba del Rey is owned by Rafael Carrión Amate, an importer of Moroccan furniture; guests can purchase most of the items in the hotel. Harking back to Moorish Al-Andalus, the seven rooms and eight suites are named after figures from Spain's Islamic era, such as Princesa Zaida and Ibn Firnas (above). We like the Beatriz de Suabia, which has a canopied thuja-wood four-poster, and a marble floor and bath. Breakfast is served under a Bedouin-style tent on the roof terrace; return here later on for a dip in the jacuzzi. There's also a massage room where you can book treatments. The inner courtyard leads to a blue-and-white-tiled tapas bar – perfect for a drink and a bite. *Calle de Bécquer 9, T 954 915 800, www.alcobadelrey.com*

Las Casas de la Judería

It may take you a while to find your room in this labyrinth of converted mansions and courtyards, but the journey is worth it. This is a charming hotel with excellent service. Room 701 (pictured) is typical of the clean, classical Spanish decor throughout. In summer, unwind in the rooftop pool.
Plaza de Santa María La Blanca 3,
T 954 415 150, www.casasypalacios.com

Hotel Alfonso XIII

The neo-Mudejar facade of this stately pile dominates the historic centre. It was commissioned in 1928 by King Alfonso XIII and provided all the necessary luxuries for visiting heads of state during the 1929 Ibero-American Expo. Today it remains at the heart of the city's social scene after a refurbishment by HBA in 2012 that returned areas like the art deco American Bar to their original elegance. Rooms, such as Junior Suite 203 (above), combine antique and modern furnishings and have lavish marble bathrooms. Linger in the lobby (opposite) to admire the period chandeliers, coffered mahogany ceiling, colourful frescoes and azulejo tiles, lounge by the open-air pool and dine in the delightfully airy courtyard (see p033).
Calle San Fernando 2, T 954 917 000, www.luxurycollection.com/alfonsoxiii

Hotel Casa 1800

Centred around an 1864 mansion-palace, which forms the reception and courtyard, this glossy addition to the hotel scene sprawls over several ancient buildings nearby, including the former studio of the legendary American painter and matador John Fulton. The decor is a striking mix of traditional Andalusian brick-, stone- and woodwork with contemporary design, fine drapery and the latest technology, as in the sumptuous Junior Suite (above). The hotel is situated on a busy thoroughfare so you may want to request a room away from the front; however, during Feria de Abril you can watch men and women riding in traditional dress along the streets to the tapas bar opposite, Bodega Santa Cruz, a local institution dubbed 'Las Columnas'.
Calle Rodrigo Caro 6, T 954 561 800, www.hotelcasa1800sevilla.com

EME Catedral Hotel

Barcelona designers Sandra Tarruella and Isabel López carved Seville's first boutique hotel out of a historic building facing the cathedral. It received a mixed reception from locals. Some welcomed its cutting-edge (for 2008) design (overleaf), others saw this as ill-suited so close to arguably the greatest Gothic church in Christendom. However, today both camps can be found enjoying a glass – be it a manzanilla or a mojito – on the series of roof terraces that have the best ecclesiastical views in town. All 60 rooms come with Bang & Olufsen TVs and rainshowers; we suggest booking a Deluxe Con Vistas (No 103; above) or, for more space and a balcony, a Grand Deluxe. Huge French windows peel back to reveal a cathedral seemingly close enough to touch.
Calle Alemanes 27, T 954 560 000, www.emecatedralhotel.com

Second-floor landing, EME Catedral Hotel

HOTELS

Corral del Rey

This restored 17th-century *casa palacio* hits the mark perfectly. Interior designer Kuky Mora-Figueroa has teamed Andalusian details with pastel colours and mod cons to produce a sophisticated contemporary boutique hotel with flair. All 13 bedrooms, including a penthouse, have Norwegian limed-oak floors, marble bathrooms and original wooden doors and windows, as well as iPod docks, Egyptian cotton sheets and wi-fi. The second-floor rooms in the main building, including Junior Suite 5 (above), feel more spacious due to the high vaulted ceilings. There is a plunge pool on the roof and a downstairs space where occasional flamenco shows are held at the request of guests. The breakfast here almost merits a stay on its own.
Calle Corral del Rey 12, T 954 227 116, www.corraldelrey.com

Las Casas del Rey de Baeza
The whitewashed facade, yellow window frames and pots of geraniums outside belie the contemporary interiors of this boutique hotel, part of the Hospes group. The tiled open-plan spaces feature a mix of textured furnishings, such as chenille sofas and woven needle-grass mats, abstract artworks and midcentury pieces, including Arne Jacobsen's 'Swan' chairs. The rooms, such as 44 (above), are well proportioned with plenty of natural light and cool stone floors, and some have walk-in wardrobes. There's a restaurant serving local cuisine, a small spa, a pool and bar on the roof, and an interior patio shaded by banana trees that provides a retreat from the merciless midday sun.
Calle Santiago 2, Plaza Jesús de la Redención, T 954 561 496, www.hospes.com

24 HOURS
SEE THE BEST OF THE CITY IN JUST ONE DAY

Our day offers a glimpse of Seville's many faces, taking you to an ornate palace (opposite) for a refined breakfast, then a stroll past the city's defining landmark, La Giralda (see p013), the baroque Palacio Arzobispal (Plaza Virgen de los Reyes) – the gateway to the Jewish quarter – and on to the magnificent Real Alcázar (see p034), which melds Mudejar and Castilian baroque architecture. Follow this with a visit to Casa de Pilatos (see p036). We suggest taking lunch at Tribeca (see p038) before viewing some modern Spanish art at the CAAC (see p039). The hammams at Aire de Sevilla (see p094) will provide a little afternoon R&R.

If you can, squeeze in more classic art at the Museo de Bellas Artes (Plaza del Museo 9, T 954 786 500), whose strong Spanish collection includes works by El Greco, Murillo and Juan de Valdés Leal. Head back along the river for two strikingly contemporary experiences, the art-space Delimbo (see p043) and the Metropol Parasol (see p044), an extraordinary high-tech hybrid canopy known locally as the 'Mushroom of the Incarnation'; climb to the top for sunset. Then head to San Vicente to feast on gourmet tapas at Eslava (see p046) and on for a digestif in fashionable Alameda (see p012). Push into the night at the eccentric El Garlochi (see p047) or the small but lively dance bar Groucho (Calle Federico Sánchez Bedoya 20, T 657 533 471). Aim to arrive here about 1am.
For full addresses, see Resources.

10.00 Hotel Alfonso XIII

Its Moorish arches and Italian marble fountain make the Alfonso's courtyard restaurant, San Fernando, a delightful setting for breakfast. This grand hotel is the favoured haunt of politicians, visiting US film stars and the glamorous, gossipy wives of the top bullfighters, so the crowd is never dull. Built in the final days of the pre-Civil War monarchy, it is an empire's last architectural gasp in wood, marble and decoration from long-gone institutions like the Real Fabrica de Tápices. In summer, come for Sunday brunch (April to October, from 1pm), a fine spread of tapas, salads and *verrines* served next to the best pool in town. It is a welcome respite from the heat in a city where temperatures in July and August can rival those in the Sahara.
Calle San Fernando 2, T 954 917 000, luxurycollection.com/alfonsoxiii

11.00 Real Alcázar

In 1248, Fernando III conquered Seville, ending Moorish rule in Al-Andalus. About a century later, in 1364, Pedro I ordered construction of a royal palace on the ruins of a 10th- to 11th-century fort, employing Moorish craftsmen. Remnants of the original architecture can be seen in the Salón de los Embajadores (Ambassadors' Hall), which has exquisite latticework and tiling, and a spectacular golden dome. Galleries and halls are decorated with tiled murals and frescoes, leading to the stunning Patio de las Doncellas. The whole complex is set in beautiful topiary gardens. View the baths of Doña María de Padilla (left) and the *Virgen de los Navegantes*, a rare depiction on canvas of Christopher Columbus, painted by Alejo Fernández in the 16th century. Columbus' remains lie entombed in the cathedral next door.
Patio de Banderas, T 954 502 324, www.alcazarsevilla.org

12.00 Casa de Pilatos
Its name derived from Pontius Pilate, the residence of the Dukes of Medinaceli, built in the early 16th century, is regarded as the first, and finest, Andalusian palace. The world-famous courtyard (above) is an astonishing mix of Italian Renaissance architecture and Moorish decor, and it is littered with sculptures of Spanish kings and Roman emperors . Used in films from *Lawrence of Arabia* to *Kingdom of Heaven*, it is in remarkable condition. However, look closely and inscribed among the scrolls in Arabic you'll find the line: 'Coca-Cola, it's the real thing', added by a hapless workman who, not knowing the language, repaired a damaged wall with lettering taken from a Moroccan coke bottle. The palace is open to the public all year round.
Plaza de Pilatos 1, T 954 225 298, www.fundacionmedinaceli.org

13.00 La Adriática

Completed in 1922, La Adriática, or Edificio Filella, was designed by the prolific local architect José Espiau y Muñoz. He gave free rein to his intricate neo-Mudejar style here, as can be seen in the detailed facade. During restoration in 2003, the white and aquamarine tiles on the dome that had been removed in the 1970s were replaced, and the colonnaded exterior was returned to its original state. The ground floor houses a pâtisserie, Confitería Filella (T 954 224 640). Espiau y Muñoz created many of Seville's best early 20th-century buildings, notably Hotel Alfonso XIII (see p017) and Edificio Pedro Roldán (Plaza del Pan), a riot of embellishment and decoration, mixing Italian gothic with the Sevillian vernacular, red-brick with blue azulejo tiles, topped by a slender cupola.
Avenida de la Constitución 2

13.30 Tribeca

On his return from working in Hong Kong, Sevillian chef Pedro Giménez decided to establish a restaurant in his home town. Tribeca opened in 2002, in an elegant, subtly lit space, with tables set around a central, circular kitchen, designed by architects Francisco Barrionuevo. Giménez's brothers Jaime and Eduardo joined up as sous chef and sommelier respectively. The menu is experimental, and sometimes includes fish caught by Giménez himself. Expect dishes such as red king prawn tartare with veal marrow and celery, or the more traditional oxtail. An adventurous wine list throws up lesser-known bottles from small bodegas; the aperitif brandies and local dessert sherries are particularly good. Closed Sundays.
Calle Chaves Nogales 3, T 954 426 000, www.restaurantetribeca.com

15.00 CAAC

Seville's delightful CAAC (Centro Andaluz de Arte Contemporáneo) is housed in the former Carthusian monastery Santa María de las Cuevas, which was founded in 1400. English merchant Charles Pickman turned it into a porcelain and earthenware factory in 1841, hence the chimney stacks, which were active until as recently as 1982. Now it provides a serene setting in which to view modern art. CAAC's permanent collection comprises works by Luis Gordillo, Candida Höfer, Rebecca Horn, Pablo Palazuelo and Joseph Kosuth, and the temporary exhibitions feature international artists, including many South Americans. The site also encompasses an orchard and a lake. CAAC is closed on Mondays and shuts its doors at 3pm on Sundays.
Avenida Américo Vespucio 2, T 955 037 070, www.caac.es

17.00 Monumento a la Tolerancia
Designed by the Basque sculptor Eduardo Chillida, this distinctive monument was inaugurated in 1992 to mark 500 years since Catholic monarchs Ferdinand and Isabella captured Granada and signed the Alhambra Decree with Emir Muhammad XII. This permitted the Moors to stay in Spain along with any Jews willing to convert to Christianity; limited 'tolerances' that were soon abandoned as the Spanish Inquisition began. A unifying sculpture based on a pair of arms outstretched from an abstract torso, it has been adopted by older locals as symbolising the horns of a bull, sited as it is opposite La Maestranza (see p014). On the riverbank near a host of sun-drenched bars, *La Tolerancia* is located at what was once the end of the route for all the gold and silver of the Americas; money that funded Spain's long reign as the world's major colonial power.
Paseo Alcalde Marqués de Contadero

041

24 HOURS

17.30 Robles Laredo

Stop for a first-rate coffee and pastry, or white wine and foie gras, at this café on the corner of Seville's famous shopping street, Calle de las Sierpes. The neo-baroque edifice was first designed by Ramón Balbuena Huertas in 1918, and added to in 1927 by Manuel Cuadrillero Sáez, before the ground floor opened as a bar in 1930. Outside seating spills on to the majestic 16th-century Plaza de San Francisco, which used to be where the Inquisition's henchmen and the early matadors, in the pre-Maestranza era, all carried out their bloody work. Laredo is now the sixth establishment owned by accomplished Sevillian restaurateur Juan Robles; his daughter Laura is the artisan responsible for its pastries.
Calle de las Sierpes 90, T 954 293 232, www.casa-robles.com

18.00 Delimbo

A cross between graffiti-art shop, street fashion store and contemporary gallery, this is a multidisciplinary creation/propagation space for urban culture in a city that has spawned street artists like Logan, Tote King and SFDK. Set in a 1919 modernist building designed by José Espiau y Muñoz, the space was taken over in 2006 by Seville street artists Laura Calvarro and Seleka Muñoz, who continue to direct it. Showing permanent and temporary exhibitions by international artists of all types, from conceptual to abstract expressionist, Delimbo also hosts events and concerts. The edgy Alfalfa area in which it is based has a lively late-night dive-bar scene, exemplified by the always-open bar Berlín (Calle de los Boteros 2).
Calle Pérez Galdós 1, T 955 294 188, www.delimbo.com

19.30 Metropol Parasol

After long delays while engineers Arup developed the technology to build it, architect Jürgen Mayer H's €90m Parasol was unveiled in 2011. Four 27m-high concrete and timber trunks support a 150m by 70m by 29m undulating lattice canopy of steel and wood, containing a walkway and a café, and covering a restored market and some Roman ruins.
Plaza de la Encarnación

24 HOURS

21.00 Eslava

Superb tapas, slick service and competitive prices have ensured popularity for the family-run Eslava since it opened in 1985. There are just seven tables, but waiting or ordering at the bar if there is a long queue keeps most punters happy. The furnishings are simple wooden shelves and tables, and blackboards announce the dishes of the day. If available, try the caramelised pork ribs cooked in honey, *boquerones rellenos* (stuffed fried anchovies) or the *salmorejo* (a dense, creamy gazpacho), and, for dessert, Eslava's orange tart. On nearby Alamada de Hércules (see p012) outdoor bars abound. Begin the evening at Cafe Ciudad Condal (T 655 557 924) with a postprandial 'gin-tonic'; Spain consumes more gin per capita than any other nation.
Calle Eslava 3, T 954 906 568, www.espacioeslava.com

24.00 El Garlochi

Hard to find, but impossible to forget once you've been (imagine a cathedral interior designed by Versace on acid), El Garlochi is a local landmark. Religious artefacts, homoerotic paintings of Christ and the saints, and velvet-draped effigies of the Virgin Madonna litter this high-camp tribute to Spanish Catholicism. Pepe, the barman and owner, will regale you with tales of the celebrities who have passed through El Garlochi's doors – look out for the cherished photo of his wife with Julio Iglesias – which is all part of this venue's charm. For a shot of liquid kitsch, order a glass of *sangre de Cristo* (blood of Christ), a heady cocktail combining champagne, red wine and gold tequila. Don't even think about turning up until after midnight, when the locals come out to play.

Calle de los Boteros 26

URBAN LIFE
CAFÉS, RESTAURANTS, BARS AND NIGHTCLUBS

Perhaps once the most staid of Spanish cities, the Seville you'll encounter today is far more modish. An injection of fresh blood from around the country and a boost in the number of enterprising locals has helped kickstart new trends in dining and design. The city's clubs and restaurants are busy innovating, and even some of Seville's most old-fashioned tapas joints have modernised their menus. However, great counter food is all about the ingredients, of course, so for the best *jamón ibérica*, head to Bar Las Teresas (Calle de Santa Teresa 2, T 954 213 069), and for larger plates, it's hard to beat Infanta (Calle de Arfe 32-36, T 954 229 689). The most creative cuisine in town is to be found at Contenedor (see p050), Vinería San Telmo (see p068) and Abantal (see p069).

Locals don't like to rush things, and will sit down to dinner late, at about 10pm. Bars tend to stay open until 3am, when the clubs begin to ramp it up. The liveliest areas for drinking are Alameda de Hércules (see p012) and around Calle de Arfe. The latter is home to popular haunts Casa Matías (No 11) and Café Boheme (No 24a), while Horacio Restaurante (Calle de Antonia Díaz 9, T 954 225 385) is round the corner. By the river, call into the upscale nightclub Sala Boss (Calle del Betis 67) in summer, and two of our favourite waterfront hangouts, the minimalist Abades Triana (see p055) and its long-term rival Puerto Delicia (see p060).
For full addresses, see Resources.

Nuevo Gastromium

After learning their trade in the kitchens of Europe, Andalusian chefs Miguel Díaz, José Luís Carabias and Ernesto Masalaña teamed up to reform what they saw as a tired tapas scene, opening Gastromium in 2009 when all were still in their twenties. It relaunched as Nuevo Gastromium in 2011, with a revamped *alta cocina sevilla* menu. The stripped-back, minimalist space was designed by the Barcelona-based Francesc Rifé Studio, a stark departure from the usual fussy Sevillian interior. Tasting menus take their cue from the black, white and gold colour palette, and sommelier Francisco Javier Ponce advises on choices from the well-stocked cellar. The high quality of the cuisine, decor and service make this restaurant a must, even if it's a little out of the way in Porvenir.
Calle Ramón Carande 12, T 954 625 555

Contenedor

This boho restaurant/diner is popular for its retro decor and imaginative cooking. Determined by what is available at the market, the creative blackboard menu can feature ox, venison or wild boar and fresh fish in sauces such as white truffle oil or vanilla, plus a healthy sprinkling of salads; regulars return for the rice with duck and mushroom. The wine list has well-chosen Andalusian options, including good reds from Ronda. Contenedor is also a bit of a scene. As well as the art exhibitions and the abstract landscapes by Sevillian painter Ricardo Llinares, arthouse films and locally made shorts are projected on to the walls, and, on Mondays, alt-cult happenings could include anything from theatrical recitals to live gigs and belly dancing.
Calle San Luis 50, T 954 916 333,
www.contenedorcultural.com

Arte y Sabor

Many of the bars and restaurants that line Alameda de Hércules (see p012) fall on the wrong side of the hip/dive divide, but this slim space with minimalist decor is a stylish oasis. Formerly one of the city's very few vegetarian restaurants, hard times led it to succumb to the desires of the local carnivores in 2011, and the menu is now somewhat confused, with reports of a few wobbles in the kitchen. Still, it remains a lovely spot to while away a sunny afternoon people-watching from the outside tables. Treat yourself to one of the tempting desserts – perhaps the chocolate volcano with nougat ice cream on a bed of white chocolate – and a lemonade made with yerba buena, or a few *tintos de verano* (red wine, tonic and ice).
Alameda de Hércules 85, T 954 372 897, www.arteysabor.es

052

La Carbonería

Seville has plenty of flamenco bars (see p059), which vary wildly in terms of the quality of performers and clientele (many are strictly for tourists only), but this is one place that does draw aficionados. Owned by the Duke of Segorbe, who also has the nearby Las Casas de la Judería (see p022) in his portfolio, this makeshift space may have no sign outside but it's pretty hard to miss. In a former coal warehouse, a corrugated fibreglass roof covers the large indoor and outdoor areas, which are both sparsely furnished with tables and long benches. Dancers, guitarists and singers perform every evening until midnight on the small stage, and the crowd fuels the atmosphere with the help of the local tipple, *vino naranja* (white wine infused with orange blossom). *Calle Levíes 18, T 954 214 460, www.levies18.com*

Hotel Doña María

This grand house near the cathedral once belonged to Samuel ha-Levi, advisor to King Pedro 'The Cruel'. After the expulsion and/or forced conversion of the Jews under Catholic rulers Ferdinand and Isabella, it came to the Marqueses de la Peña, whose descendants turned it into an old-fashioned hotel in 1965, with the innovation of a roof terrace (above), complete with a pool. The Escher-like convolutions formed from its haphazard buttressing become even more fascinating after a glass of the dangerously easy-to-drink *agua de sevilla* (despite the name, water is the least of its ingredients, which include cava, whisky, Cointreau and pineapple juice). After refurbishment in 2010, its outdoor sofas make it far more comfortable than its parvenu competitors.
Calle Don Remondo 19, T 954 224 990, www.hdmaria.com

Abades Triana

The first in a string of riverside venues created waves from its opening in 2009, and Seville's high society still flocks to this glass pavilion topped by an oxidised steel awning. The dining room carries the trademarks of designer Jaime Montaner of local firm Demópolis, who used floor-to-ceiling windows to give each table a serene view. Take an aperitif on the terrace, looking back over the river to the historic centre, from the squat bullring in the foreground to the steeples and domes scattered across the backdrop. Then dine on steak tartare or suckling lamb with couscous prepared by chefs Elías del Toro and Óscar Fernández. Wash it down with a rioja *reserva*, which are at least a year older than the two-year-old *crianzas*.
Calle del Betis 69a, T 954 286 459, www.abadestriana.com

Sol y Sombra

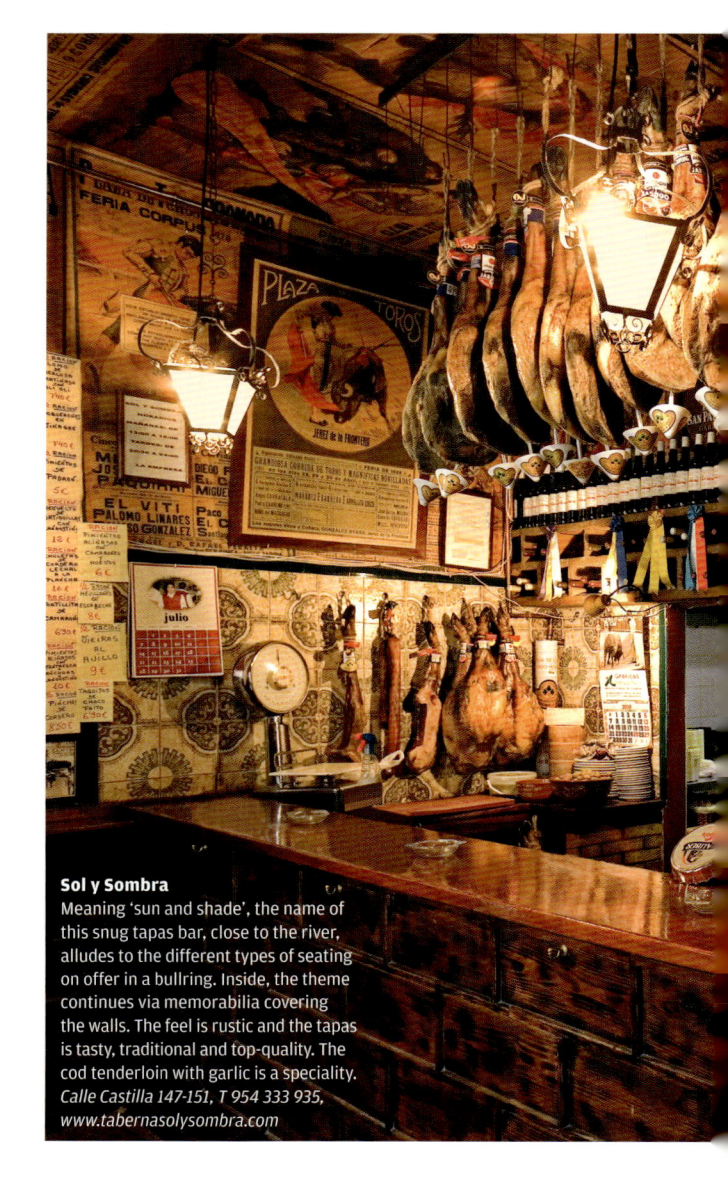

Meaning 'sun and shade', the name of this snug tapas bar, close to the river, alludes to the different types of seating on offer in a bullring. Inside, the theme continues via memorabilia covering the walls. The feel is rustic and the tapas is tasty, traditional and top-quality. The cod tenderloin with garlic is a speciality.
Calle Castilla 147-151, T 954 333 935, www.tabernasolysombra.com

URBAN LIFE

República Café

The creation of Sevillian interior designer Ernesto de Ceano, this laidback glass-cube café is big with the laptop brigade, but not solely thanks to its free wi-fi. Two large screen-printed panels dominate the dining area (above), and the white lounge is furnished with Lievore Altherr Molina's 'Catifa' chairs, from Arper. Perch on one of the Viccarbe stools at the bar, which is open until 3am, and soak up the geek-chic scene. If you are feeling peckish, there are gourmet burgers, bocadillos and Mediterranean-style tapas on offer. Eye candy is often provided by República's famously handsome waiters.
Alameda de Hércules 27, T 954 909 435, www.republicacafesevilla.blogspot.com

Los Gallos

The trouble with authentic flamenco (born of loss and sadness and performed in homes, gypsy encampments and bars that can never be found twice) is its irregularity. *Duende*, the untranslatable 'dark spirit' at its heart, doesn't wear a watch or exist on a map. However, the best flamenco 'show', or *tablao*, in Seville, the city at the heart of this artform, is Los Gallos (The Cockerels). Don't be put off by the simple seating and stage dressed with a blacksmith's forge. The painted roosters behind do not strut with more swagger, nor posture with more staccato purity than the dancers here, inspired by the 'black sounds' that the singers and guitarists conjure. Two-hour shows start at 8pm and 10.30pm, and have run since 1966.
Plaza de Santa Cruz 11, T 954 216 981, www.tablaolosgallos.com

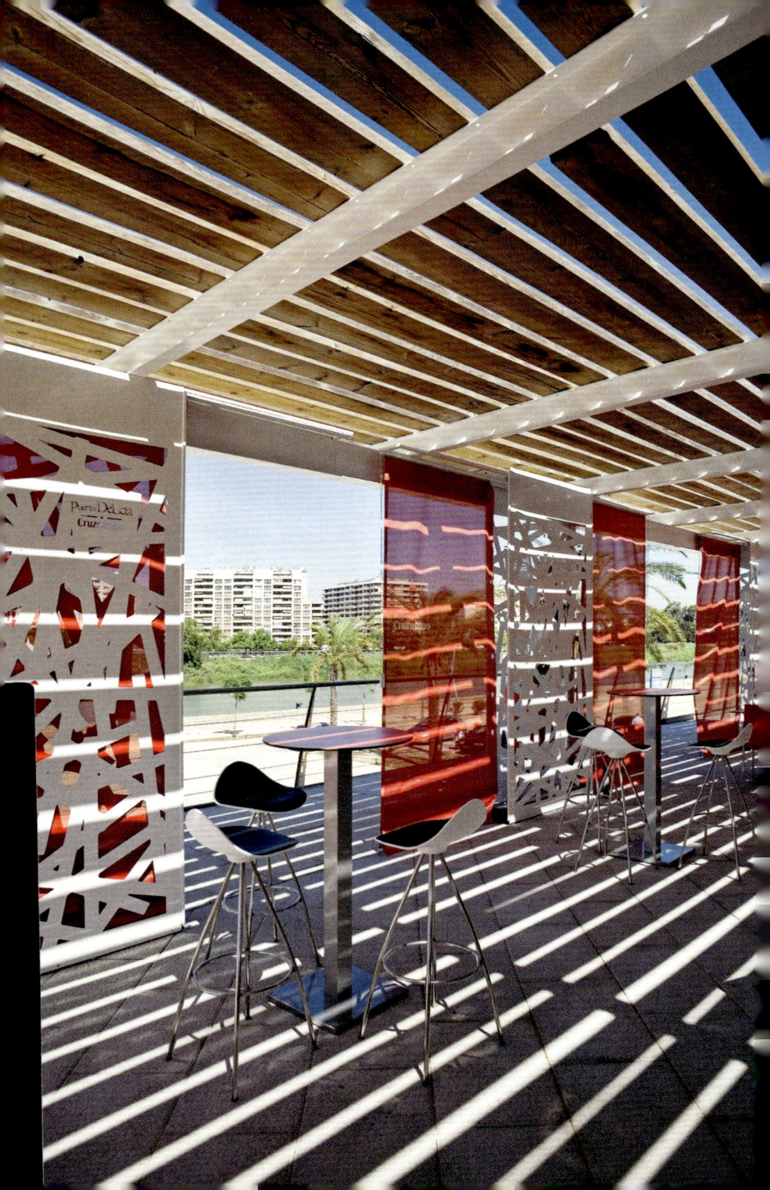

Puerto Delicia

Part of a major riverfront regeneration project that has since foundered as funds dried up, Puerta Delicia is the success story and delivers much more than your average waterside eaterie. You can moor your yacht 20m from the door, and in the glass-fronted downstairs dining area (above), designer Ernesto de Ceano has created a classy space featuring 'Mollie' seating and 'Infinity' lamps by Catalan designers Vibia. The upstairs Quiosca Delicia seafood bar is decked out with Allermuir furniture, and the champagne bar (opposite) offers great views. Chef Antonio Bort has made a name for himself here. Order simple dishes such as the catch of the day or have a blowout with the suckling pig in beetroot stew (in season).
Muelle de las Delicias, T 955 115 656, www.puertodelicia.es

Zelai

This gem was opened by Sevillian Paloma Valenzuela, and Xabier Lavado, from San Sebastian, in 2008, at the inception of the new-wave tapas movement. Provenance is taken seriously and livestock is sourced from the owners' friends' farms. Many of the dishes have an Asian twist; we suggest the hake in black tempura with asparagus, the ox sirloin, or the hunks of *presa ibérica* with Thai vegetables – unlike in old-school tapas joints, vegetables don't die by frying pan here. The narrow space has a striking geometric design by local architects Alt-q, who unified the bar and restaurant with an angular, ribbed wooden installation. We like to dine standing at the counter to watch the ebb and flow of young urbanites catching up at full volume.
Calle de Albareda 22, T 954 229 992, www.restaurantezelai.com

URBAN LIFE

Jaylu

Always packed, this restaurant is said to serve some of the best shrimp in Spain, renowned for the fastidious way in which it is prepared and presented. The clientele includes famous *toreros* and well-heeled locals, and the traditional interior, which was furnished by local designers Guadarte, adds to the decidedly Andalusian vibe. Star chef Ferran Adrià said he considers Jaylu to be one of the best restaurants in Seville and pops by whenever he's in town. If you don't wish to sit down to the full-on extravaganza, order some tapas at the bar to sample the signature shrimp, sent from the ports of Huelva and Cadiz.
Calle López de Gomara 19, T 954 339 476, www.restaurantejaylu.com

El Tendido

Hotel Colón has long provided respite for the bullfighters from La Maestranza (see p014) — it rents rooms for the half day for them to change into their golden 'suit of lights', and matador photos are part of the decor. It was bought by the Meliá Group and upgraded with the help of Philippe Starck and Marcel Wanders in 2010, and the hotel bar, El Tendido, is now named after the stands in the bullring. Relax with a cocktail, and sample the small plates and confectionery created by Francisco Torreblanca, one of the world's top pastry chefs, as you watch fans wait for their heroes to appear after the evening battle. Or arrive late afternoon to see matadors grim-faced and pale in the lobby before heading out for their date with destiny. *Gran Meliá Colón, Calle Canalejas 1, T 954 505 599, www.gran-melia-colon.com*

Antique Theatro
Set within the Olympic pavilion built for Expo 92 (hence the marble colonnades), this upscale lounge/club opens late on weekends in warmer months only, and the door policy is tough. It's more louche in summer when it's called Aqua Antique and the action moves to the outdoor booths overlooking the pool (pictured).
Calle Matemáticos Rey Pastor y Castro, T 954 462 207, www.antiquetheatro.com

URBAN LIFE

Vinería San Telmo

When Argentine Juan Manuel Tarquini came to Seville in 2004, everyone was making the same half-dozen tapas dishes. He set out to do something different — in atmosphere and cuisine — and together with his pastry-chef wife, Reyes Moreno Bejarano, created a charming space, with a distinctive tiled floor, rough orange-red walls and photos by Tarquini himself. Following the addition of head chef José Vicente Flores, the place established itself as a lunchtime favourite, but is a great bet at any time. We love the *pluma ibérica*, which is cooked like rump steak and has the sweet tang of the acorn forests where the pigs are reared. Pair it with a bottle from the glass cellar, stocked with little-known wines brought from across Spain.
Paseo Catalina de Ribera 4, T 954 410 600, www.vineriasantelmo.com

Abantal

Architects Jaime Márquez and Santiago Pérez have crafted an interior that manages to be modern and inviting, thanks to warm pine floors and a bar/waiting area in which the lights are dimmed as the night progresses. The cooking is a hit too, a result of award-winning chef Julio Fernández Quintero's fusion of Andalusian and Arab cuisine. The seasonal ingredients are top quality and his use of spices is appealingly subtle. Another plus is Abantal's wine list (try the reasonably priced pairing menu), a credit to sommelier Santiago de la Higuera's talent for sourcing excellent bottles from small Spanish producers.
Alcalde José de la Bandera 7-9,
T 954 540 000, www.abantalrestaurante.es

INSIDER'S GUIDE
ÁNGEL LUIS CARMONA, MATADOR

A bullfighter since he was just 14, Ángel Luis Carmona became a full matador in 2008. He lives in nearby Osuna and, like all in his profession, is often on the road, yet he's always drawn back to Seville. 'You bump into people you know all the time,' he says. 'And it's so beautiful in spring when the orange trees are in blossom.'

After breakfast of toast with tomato paste and serrano ham and fresh Sevillian orange juice at Carmela (Calle Santa María la Blanca 6, T 954 540 590), it's time for cape training in Parque de María Luisa (see p088). Carmona has lunch in Casa Pepe Hillo (Calle de Adriano 24, T 954 564 145), named after the legendary 19th-century matador. 'It's got more bulls' heads than anywhere else – quite an achievement. I love the pork loin cooked in whisky.' Over the road is the matadors' tailor and purveyor of leather goods, Pedro Algaba (Calle de Adriano 9, T 955 091 511). If Carmona has a friend in the ring that evening, he'll say a prayer for him in the bullfighters' church, Basílica de la Macarena (Calle de Bécquer 1).

On days when there is no corrida, he heads to Casa Matías (see p048) for the flamenco guitar and singers, before dining on tapas at Hijos de E Morales (Calle García de Vinuesa 11, T 954 221 242), and perhaps a nightcap in the azulejo-tiled Casa Anselma (Calle Pagés del Corro 49), when the action starts around midnight. 'The owner is one of Seville's best flamenco performers,' he says.

For full addresses, see Resources.

071

URBAN LIFE

ARCHITOUR
A GUIDE TO SEVILLE'S ICONIC BUILDINGS

Expo 92 heralded a change in direction for Sevillian architecture. The calibre of the contributors – Tadao Ando, Santiago Calatrava, Imre Makovecz, Nicholas Grimshaw, Jean-Paul Viguier and Bing Thom, to name a few – and the success of their buildings brought a new confidence to the city. Today, only a few of these pavilions survive, such as Pabellón de Finlandia (opposite) and Pabellón de la Navegación (Camino de los Descubrimientos 2, T 954 043 111). The latter was designed by Spanish architect Guillermo Vázquez Consuegra, who also renovated the monastery in La Cartuja to include the Centro Andaluz de Arte Contemporáneo (see p039).

Legacies of the city's Moorish past can be seen in the early 20th-century neo-Mudejar buildings and squares built as part of architect Aníbal González's urban development plan. La Adriática (see p037), and the Plaza de España and Hotel Alfonso XIII (see p024), which were both completed for the 1929 Ibero-American Exposition, are the most important examples.

More recently, Seville has been meeting the challenges of its growing population and popularity. A rethink of its public spaces (notably the waterfront) and major transport systems resulted in a Rafael Moneo-designed terminal at San Pablo Airport in 1992, a tram network in 2007, and in 2009 the first line of a new metro. The city's 21st-century metropolitan image is taking shape.

For full addresses, see Resources.

Pabellón de Finlandia

The work of Monark, a group of students (Juha Jääskeläinen, Juha Kaakko, Petri Rouhiainen, Matti Sanaksenaho and Jari Tirkkonen) from the Otaniemi School of Architecture in Helsinki, who were all under 28, this arresting design was based on a canyon in central Finland nicknamed the Shaft of Hell. The structure comprises an oxidised steel 'box' connected by a short open bridge to a separate pine-clad building (above), which was constructed using techniques employed in traditional Finnish shipbuilding. The juxtaposition of the organic and the industrial across the narrow 15m-deep divide creates a pleasing dramatic tension. Visitors voted the pavilion one of the best entries in the Expo. Currently, it houses the architectural research foundation, FIDAS.
Calle Marie Curie 3, www.fidas.es

San Ignacio de Loyola
Completed in 1963, during Seville's building boom, this striking concrete church in San Pablo was initially viewed by locals as an eyesore. Fifty years on, the structure, by architects Luis Recasens and Antonio Peña with painter Santiago del Campo, is deservedly regarded as visionary. The modernist aesthetic is continued in the spartan interior.
Avenida de Pedro Romero, T 954 518 727

ARCHITOUR

075

Cibercentro Macarena Tres Huertas
On the site of a former basketball court and surrounded by eight-floor residential blocks, this gleaming wi-fi centre and event space was intended as an inspirational gathering point in this deprived and less than salubrious part of town. Working to a tight budget, architects Mediomundo raised a concrete-and-glass cube, wrapped in lacquered steel, above an artificial-grass plaza that is teched-up to allow online access, even when the venue is closed. Inside are computer labs, meeting rooms, a café, and an enclosed roof terrace with river views; ventilation and shading is regulated by angled 'gills'. It's a witty intervention – the colour derives from the Spanish word for the internet, *la red*. The real shame is that the centre has had to be fenced in to guard against vandalism.
Calle José Díaz

Torre Triana

This hulking 1993 government office block in La Cartuja was designed by Francisco Javier Sáenz de Oíza, architect of a number of remarkable buildings in Spain. Among them are Madrid's organic, mushroom-like 1968 Torres Blancas apartment block and the 1989 Centro Atlántico de Arte Moderno in Gran Canaria, a delightfully considered reworking of a former palace. Sáenz de Oíza's expressiveness marked a sharp departure from the neoclassical aesthetic that had prevailed under Franco. Here, between the Guadalquivir and the canal, Torre Triana's squat marble-block facade is pierced by galleon-style windows, and the two funnels that poke from the circular roof echo those of an ocean liner. It was inspired by the work of Estonian-American architect Louis Kahn.
Calle Juan Antonio de Vizarrón

Estación de Santa Justa
Completed in 1991 and designed by local architects Cruz y Ortiz, Seville's sleek railway hub has become the third-busiest station in Spain. Lines linking Seville with Cordoba, Malaga and Madrid (by AVE train this trip takes two-and-a-half hours) converge here. The pared-down interior makes maximum use of natural light, and 'inside-out' vents help reduce the noise levels and draw cool air into the departure area; it is a coherent design based on principles of flow and circulation. The 80,000 sq m complex was built in what was a previously undeveloped part of the city centre, but the attempt to create a new urban nucleus has been less successful. Cruz y Ortiz also designed the Maritime Museum in Cadiz in 1989, and the Spanish pavilion for the Expo 2000 in Hanover.
Avenida de Kansas City, T 954 537 626

ARCHITOUR

SHOPPING
THE BEST RETAIL THERAPY AND WHAT TO BUY

Seville's lively, colourful markets are some of the best in Spain. The covered Mercado de Triana near the Puente de Isabel II, and the market on Calle Feria, which is one of the oldest in the city, are both excellent places to find fresh produce; Calle Feria also has a good fleamarket, El Jueves, held on Thursday mornings. Alternatively, visit the gypsy-run Mercadillo del Parque Alcosa early on a Sunday, where you can pick up antiques and ceramics.

El Arenal and Santa Cruz are the shopping hot zones; Calle de las Sierpes and Calle de la Cuna are home to the big brands. For boutiques, like El Caballo (Calle de Antonia Díaz 7, T 954 218 127) and Arsenale (see p084), explore the area around Calle de Adriano and Calle Arenal. Check out the furniture at Manuel Gavira (see p082) and for more fashion head to tailor O'Kean (Plaza Nueva 13, T 954 229 963) and designer Victorio & Lucchino (Calle de las Sierpes 86, T 954 227 951). Also pop into Agua de Sevilla (Calle Rodrigo Caro 16, T 954 564 031) for its orange-blossom perfumes.

Tierra Nuestra (Calle Constancia 41, T 954 452 119) and La Alacena de San Eloy (Calle de San Eloy 31, T 954 215 580) are the places to stock up on sherry – the latter has a wine bar where you can sample the wares, as well as gourmet delights. Andalusia is also the birthplace of flamenco, of course. Try on a pair of *zapatos de baile* (dancing shoes) or a dress at Aurora Gaviño (see p086). *For full addresses, see Resources.*

Isadora
Run by the charming Lorena Losada, this breezy, high-ceilinged shop in Santa Cruz has a whimsical, retro feel, and remains a popular port of call for young boho-chic *sevillanas*. Pleasingly, Spanish labels are well represented here; on the racks you'll find Catalan designers Skunkfunk and Malahierba, Madrid's Kling and PepaLoves from Malaga, as well as off-the-wall imports such as Sweden's Rules by Mary. Jewellery comes from independent brands like La Marelle, Lady Desidia, Krize and LindoRon; also on sale are Losada's range of fascinators, El Tocador de Isadora. Interiors feature exposed brickwork, 1920s-style wall lamps and a chandelier, and ceramic wood-effect flooring. The building itself was one of the last works by architect José Espiau y Muñoz (see p037).
Calle Pérez Galdós 1, T 954 222 750

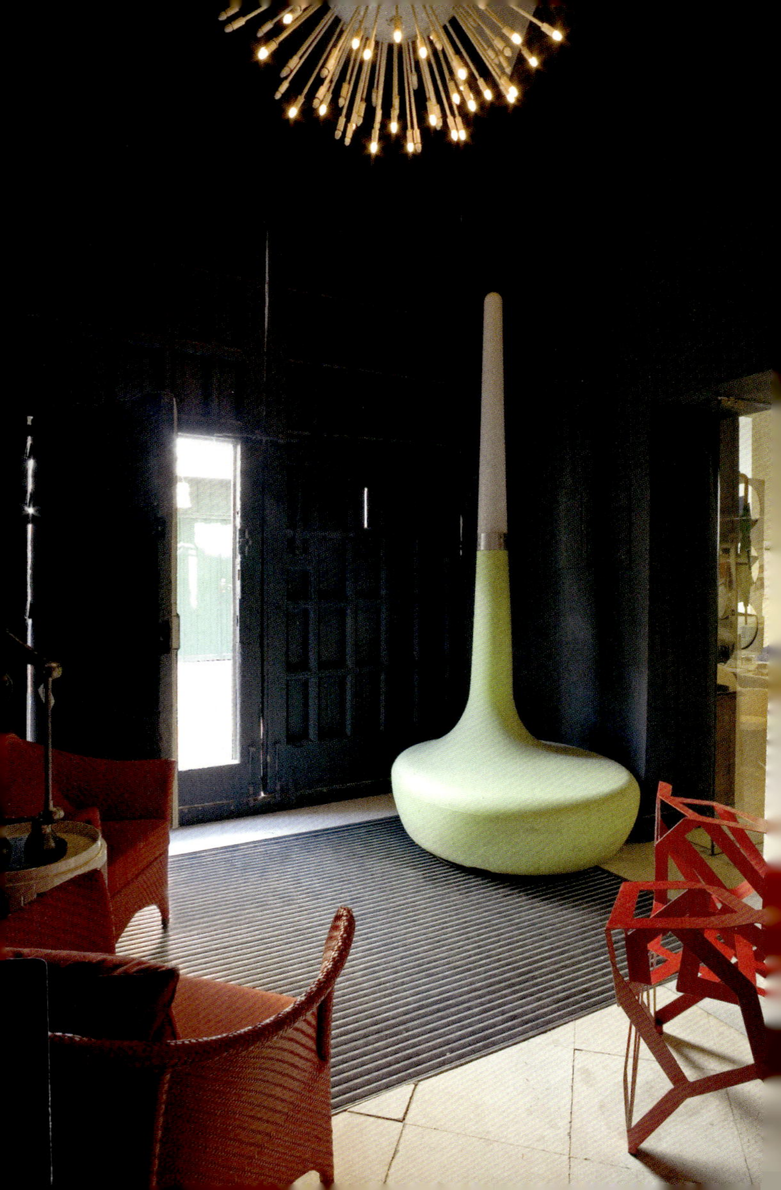

Manuel Gavira

Located in an Andalusian townhouse behind La Maestranza (see p014), just off Calle de Adriano, Manuel Gavira sells Spanish antiques, mostly 18th- or 19th-century, alongside covetable midcentury-modern European and American pieces, and contemporary furniture by the likes of Philippe Starck, Ingo Maurer and Valencian Javier Mariscal. On our visit, we spied an art deco cocktail cabinet by Jean Dunand, and an Axel Vervoordt slate table. Open since 1995, the shop is also a showroom for the work of its namesake, Spanish interior and furniture designer Manuel Gavira, whose studio, now helmed by his son Bruno, is housed in the same building.
Calle Gracia Fernández Palacios 3, T 954 226 703, www.manuelgavira.com

Arsenale

Alicia Simon has been making hats for as long as she can remember. She opened this boutique in 2007 after studying in Pisa, and it was after her favourite cinema in the town that the shop was named (not, despite some debate and a court case, the English football team). She designs for men and women, as well as stocking the French label Céline Robert, the Italian brand Borsalino, famous for its fedoras, and the Sydney-based Helen Kaminsky. Simon's creations range from modern to retro, and are mostly handmade in Seville; the bespoke millinery service is a hit with fashionable locals and in-the-know visitors. In 2013, Arsenale expanded into a second premises next door, selling a fine selection of ladies' shoes, dresses, coats, jewellery, and snake- and python-skin handbags.
Calle de Adriano 22, T 954 227 809

Lustau sherry
One of Spain's top sherry bodegas, Lustau dates from 1896 and is named after Don Emilio Lustau Ortega, the son-in-law of founder Don José Ruiz-Berdejo y Veyan. Lustau blends yields from various harvests, which are aged in the vast temperature-controlled cellars of its bodega in Jerez (T 956 341 597). We like its *almacenista* (independent-maker) sherries, and the sweet East India Solera (above), which has a rich, raisiny flavour. In Seville, you can order a small selection of Lustau sherries at Enoteca Andana (T 954 454 176), but try to find the time to make the one-hour trip south to Jerez. The epicentre of the region's sherry production is also where the famed Andalusian equestrian 'dance' is performed at the Real Escuela Andaluza del Arte Ecuestre (see p096).
www.lustau.es

Aurora Gaviño

Inspired by a night at La Carbonería (see p052), you might be tempted to splurge on a genuine flamenco dress. If so, head to this upscale boutique, a haunt of the area's many dancers. The contemporary designs are by Aurora Gaviño, who plays with the traditional gypsy look, embellishing her dresses with beads or tiny jewels, raising hemlines and plunging necklines to push the boundaries of flamenco fashion. You can also pick up shoes and fans here. This is where you'll find locals looking for an outfit for the Feria de Abril extravaganza, the high point of Seville's social calendar. Aurora Gaviño has a second branch (T 954 225 494), also located in Santa Cruz.
Calle Blanca de los Ríos 1, T 954 211 069, www.auroragavino.com

Botellas y Latas

Translated as 'bottles and tins', this tiny, old-fashioned gourmet deli is packed with a wide range of local and imported foods, heaps of aromatic spices, Andalusian wines, cavas and Spanish liqueurs. Also sold in bottles are tasty Spanish olive oils (owner Carlos Calzada is an expert) and all manner of sauces; there are more than 30 varieties of tinned paté. The regional cheeses and meats, such as the cured *pata negra* hams, are delicious. The store is situated on pedestrianised Calle Regina, a stroll from the Metropol Parasol (see p044). On the second Saturday of the month, all the traders throw open their doors and sell their wares outside, from antiques and kitsch to contemporary interior design, and, of course, gastronomy.
Calle Regina 15, T 954 293 122,
www.elclubdelgourmet.es

SPORTS AND SPAS
WORK OUT, CHILL OUT OR JUST WATCH

Seville has done a good job of increasing pedestrian zones and ridding the centre of congestion, which makes it a pleasant place to amble around. Urban planners have also created a network of cycle paths and provided a ubiquitous bike-hire scheme. Many leisure pursuits are water-based – trips along the Guadalquivir, like those run by Cruceros Torre del Oro (Paseo Alcalde Marqués de Contadero, T 954 561 692), are popular. To sail independently, head downriver to the marina of Puerto Gelves (Autovía Sevilla-Coria del Río km3.5, T 955 761 212), which is sheltered from the Atlantic tides, or hire a catamaran, kayak, pedalo or rowing boat from one of the yacht clubs lining the river. The adventurous may want to play a game of canoe water polo at Club Sevillano de Piragüismo (Paseo Marqués de Contadero, T 954 213 997).

The lush Parque de María Luisa (Avenida de María Luisa) draws joggers and in-line skaters, and Parque del Alamillo (Cortijo de Alamillo) is popular for its fitness circuit, as well as the odd sight of aspiring *toreros* training with the *carretilla*, bullhorns mounted on a unicycle. Those with plus fours should head to the Real Club de Golf (Autovía Sevilla-Utrera km3.2, T 954 124 301). Padel, a Latin American sport that combines tennis and squash, has taken off here – perhaps catch a game from the terrace at Solo Padel (Calle La Red Diecisiete 53, T 955 119 404), which has four outdoor courts. *For full addresses, see Resources.*

Epona

The art of horse riding is intricately linked with Andalusian culture. This equestrian centre between Seville and Carmona is housed in an attractive 16th-century hacienda run by Guatemalan architect Fernando García and his Scottish wife Jane, and offers rides through the area's wheat and sunflower fields, olive groves and orange orchards. Longer jaunts will take you to the sand dunes and beaches of the Parque Nacional de Doñana. There are also facilities for showjumping and dressage. To further your rural Andalusia experience, head to Cortijo de Arenales (T 955 957 048), a bull-breeding ranch in Morón de la Frontera, where you can watch displays of bullfighting on horseback and junior matadors in training.
Hacienda Los Nietos, Autovía N-IV km519, T 954 148 293, www.eponaspain.com

Carmen Navarro

If you've been partying until the early hours, local-style, a trip to this beauty one-stop for a little buffing and scrubbing should bring back your glow. An outpost of the long-established Madrid chain, Carmen Navarro is a sleek white space shot with hot pink that draws *sevillanas* (although men are most welcome too) for its comprehensive list of preening and pampering packages, from jetlag rejuvenators to facials, toning, detox and exfoliation treatments, although you'll need to book an appointment for a private consultation first. Also on offer here are more serious lifting and depigmentation anti-ageing procedures.
*Calle Rosario 4, T 954 219 379,
www.carmennavarro.com*

Despacio

This 2008 opening on the ground floor of the EME Catedral Hotel (see p027) quickly gained a reputation as the best day spa in town. Following the fusion design of the rest of the hotel – ancient and modern, Moorish and Castilian – architects Isabel López and Sandra Tarruella crafted this contemporary space without deviating from the original building's history and style. The extensive list of treatments complements this; beauty packages range from basic exfoliation to high-level oxygen and collagen technologies; also on offer are all manner of massage techniques, as well as hydrotherapy and frost jets, and Turkish bathing with chromatherapy. Once you are detoxed and polished, head up to the hotel's array of sunny roof terraces.
Calle Alemanes 25, T 954 560 000, www.emecatedralhotel.com

Estadio Benito Villamarín
The city has two Primera Liga teams, Sevilla and Real Betis, and the latter play in this 56,500-seater, expanded by architect Antonio Gonzáles Cordón in 2000. The south stand is all that remains of the original stadium, built for the 1929 Expo. The pitch is blessed before games, and kick-off is heralded by fireworks.
Avenida Heliópolis, T 902 191 907,
www.realbetisbalompie.es

SPORTS

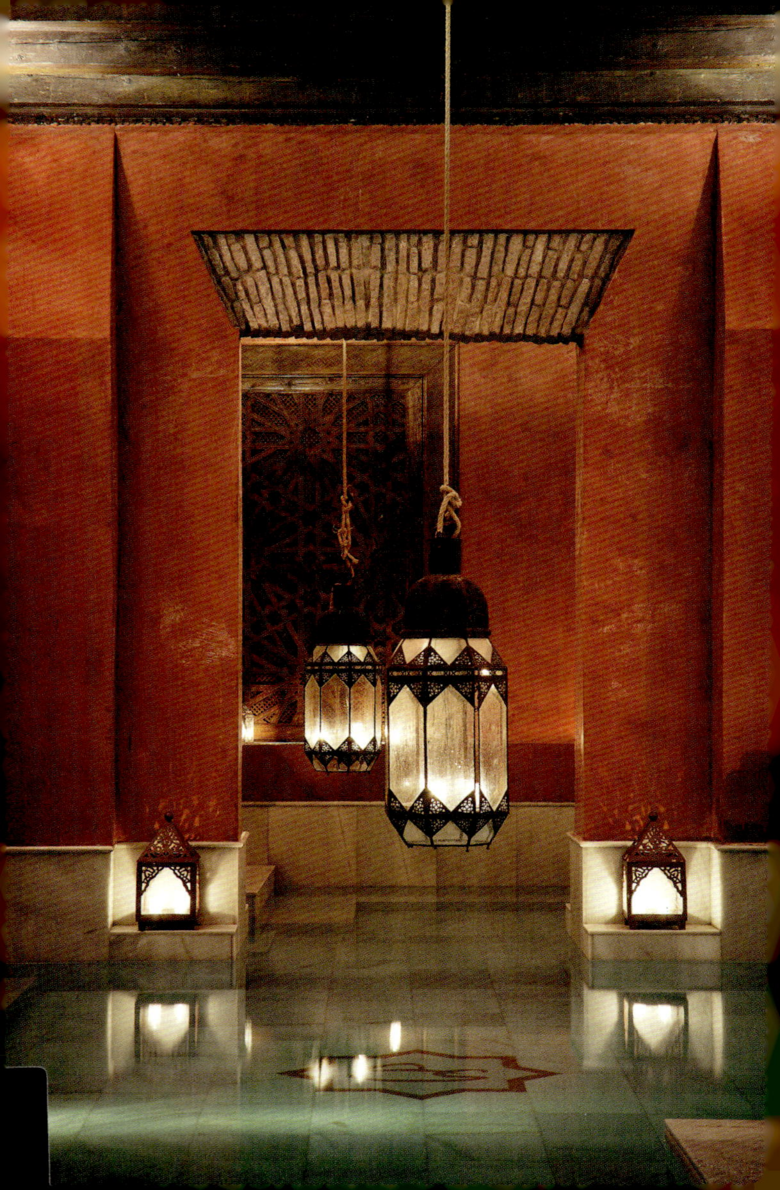

Aire de Sevilla

Originally Roman baths, then a hammam, these *baños arabes* ended up as a 16th-century palace before the current owners (the Osborne family of sherry, brandy and roadside bull silhouette fame) restored the pools and steam rooms. Behind the nondescript facade, a courtyard opens on to a terrace laid out with Moroccan tiles, where mint tea or alcohol is served as you wait your turn below. There, in cavernous spaces converted into various relaxation areas, like the warm water bath (opposite), as well as steam and treatment rooms, you can choose between myriad massages and sensory practices such as aromatherapy or fangotherapy, aka the mud bath. Or simply kick back among the carved wooden tables and goatskin seats in the tea room (above). *Calle del Aire 15, T 955 010 024, www.airedesevilla.com*

ESCAPES
WHERE TO GO IF YOU WANT TO LEAVE TOWN

Andalusia offers an impressive variety of exemplary day trips. A 140km drive to the north-east of Seville, the once-thriving Moorish capital Cordoba (see p100) and its mosque-turned-cathedral ought to be a mandatory stop on any itinerary. It's another two hours or so south-east to Granada and its sprawling Alhambra, a complex of palaces, fortresses and gardens that was home to the kings of the Nasrid dynasty. From December to April, you can ski in the nearby Sierra Nevada, whose highest peak reaches 3,482m.

We would also recommend an overnight stay amid southern Andalusia's sunflower-strewn plains, in a country hotel such as the bougainvillea-clad Hacienda de San Rafael (Apartado 28, Carretera N-IV km594, La Cabezas de San Juan, T 954 227 116). From here, continue on to Jerez de la Frontera, for its lively restaurants and bars, the illustrious Fundación Real Escuela Andaluza del Arte Ecuestre (Avenida Duque de Abrantes, T 956 319 635) and sherry bodegas like Emilio Lustau (see p085). To the west is Sanlúcar de Barrameda, a charming port that is famous for the production of manzanilla sherry, which has a flavour reminiscent of tea; sample it at Bodegas Barbadillo (Calle Virgen de Gracia y Esperanza, T 956 385 521). Watch the sun set on Bajo de Guía beach, before heading to one of the atmospheric tapas restaurants on the square – Casa Balbino (Plaza del Cabildo 14, T 956 360 513) is good for seafood. *For full addresses, see Resources.*

Torres de Hércules, Los Barrios
Madrid architect Rafael de La-Hoz's 2009 towers overlooking the Bay of Algeciras were inspired by the Pillars of Hercules on the Andalusian coat of arms. Symbolising the narrow entrance to the nearby Strait of Gibraltar, the cylinders rise from a pool of water and are wrapped in a distinctive reinforced-concrete lattice that forms the letters (if you squint hard enough) of the sailors' ancient warning, *Non Plus Ultra* (nothing further beyond). Set back by 80cm from the exterior skeleton are 20 storeys of glass-walled offices, linked by skyways, with a restaurant on the top floor. The facade continues up to 100m, ringing a roof terrace, from where you can see Africa. An antenna cheekily takes the total height of the building up to 126m, to ensure it tops La Giralda (see p013) in Seville.
Las Marismas de Palmones

Finca Cortesin, Marbella

About 220km south-east of Seville, this 215-hectare country estate hosts a hotel, golf course and spa, and has 67 spacious suites inspired by traditional Andalusian architecture. There are four swimming pools, including an elegant 50m outdoor option (above), while thermal and Turkish baths in the spa offer alternative means of relaxation. Marginally more strenuous activity plays out on the landscaped golf course, a former host venue of the Volvo World Match Play tournament. Try to tear yourself away to the nearby historical city of Ronda. The beautiful hillside *pueblo blanco* (white town) is famous for its 1793 Puente Nuevo ('New' Bridge) that passes 120m above a canyon, providing some of Spain's most dramatic mountain scenery.
*Carretera de Casares, Casares,
T 952 937 800, www.fincacortesin.com*

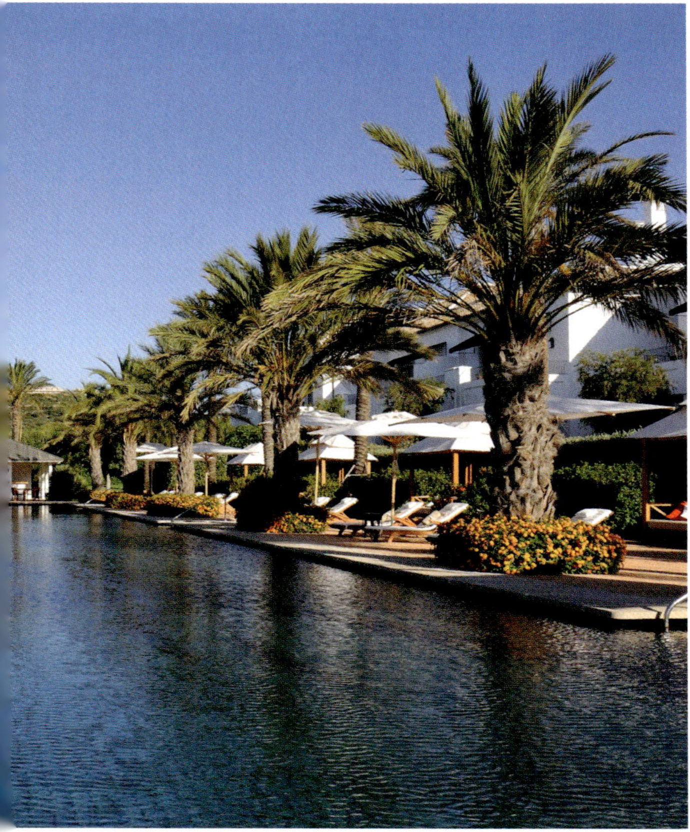

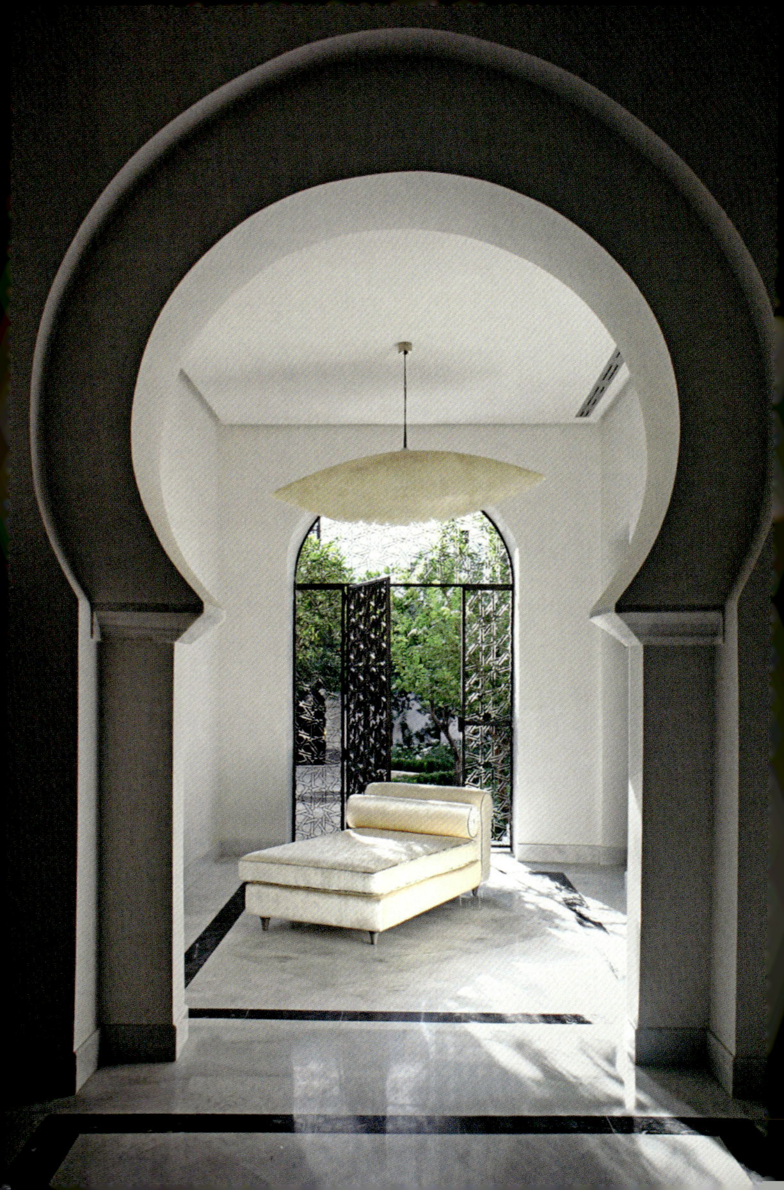

Palacio del Bailio, Cordoba
For a city conquered by the Spanish in 1236, Cordoba retains a strikingly Islamic atmosphere. It was one of the key cultural and fiscal centres of Moorish Al-Andalus, and its great mosque, the Mezquita, dates from the 8th century and has exquisite prayer rooms. After the Reconquest it was converted to a cathedral and modified architecturally up until the 18th century. In contrast, the city's periphery is home to various contemporary buildings by Rafael de La-Hoz (see p097), who was born here. We suggest staying at Palacio del Bailío, a boutique hotel set in a 16th-century palace. Rooms, such as the Deluxe (above), combine the ancient and the modern; as does the Bodyna Spa, which offers treatments among Roman ruins.
Ramirez de las Casas Deza 10-12,
T 957 498 993, www.hospes.com

Gemasolar, Fuentes de Andalucia
Much of Andalusia receives more than 300 days of sunshine a year, making the region ideal for the production of solar power, of which Spain is a world leader. The parched countryside around Seville is home to two futuristic facilities that wouldn't look out of place at NASA. Some 18km west of the city is the Planta Solar complex at Sanlúcar la Mayor, where the world's first commercial solar-power tower was built in 2007. To the east, 67km away, and visible from the road to Cordoba (see p100) is Gemasolar (right), which, at 140m, is the tallest structure in Andalusia. A mirror field of 2,650 heliostats spread over 195 hectares tracks the sun and reflects light to the top of the tower, heating molten salt up to 565°C. This can then be stored for up to 15 hours, enabling the plant to generate electricity 24 hours a day. Gemasolar began operation in 2011, and provides power to 25,000 homes.
Carretera A-4 km475

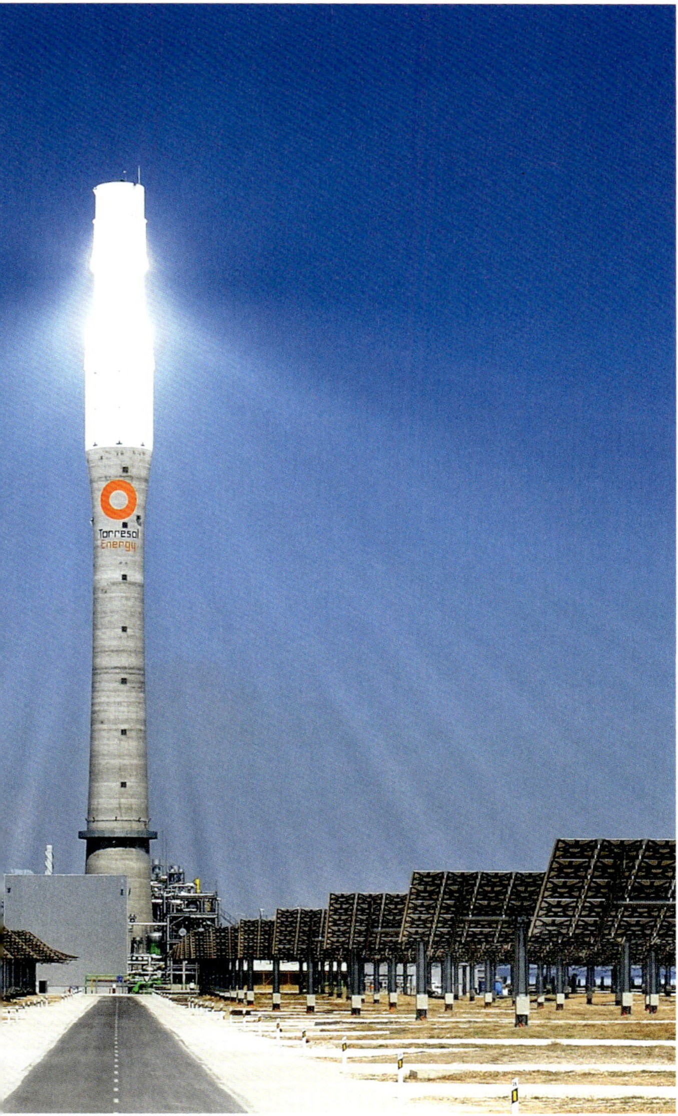
Torresol
Energy

NOTES
SKETCHES AND MEMOS

RESOURCES
CITY GUIDE DIRECTORY

A

Abades Triana 055
Calle del Betis 69a
T 954 286 459
www.abadestriana.com

Abantal 069
Alcalde José de la Bandera 7-9
T 954 540 000
www.abantalrestaurante.es

La Adriática 037
Avenida de la Constitución 2

Agua de Sevilla 080
Calle Rodrigo Caro 16
T 954 564 031
www.aguadesevilla.es

Aire de Sevilla 094
Calle del Aire 15
T 955 010 024
www.airedesevilla.com

La Alacena de San Eloy 080
Calle de San Eloy 31
T 954 215 580
www.laalacenatienda.com

Antique Theatro 066
Calle Matemáticos Rey Pastor y Castro
T 954 462 207
www.antiquetheatro.com

Arsenale 084
Calle de Adriano 22
T 954 227 809
www.arsenale.es

Arte y Sabor 051
Alameda de Hércules 85
T 954 372 897
www.arteysabor.es

Aurora Gaviño 086
Calle Blanca de los Ríos 1
T 954 211 069
Calle de Álvarez Quintero 16
T 954 225 494
www.auroragavino.com

B

Bar Las Teresas 048
Calle de Santa Teresa 2
T 954 213 069

Basílica de la Macarena 070
Calle de Bécquer 1

Berlín 043
Calle de los Boteros 2

Bodegas Barbadillo 096
Calle Virgen de Gracia y Esperanza
Sanlúcar de Barrameda
T 956 385 521
www.barbadillo.net

Bodegas Lustau 085
Arcos 53
Jerez de la Frontera
T 956 341 597
www.lustau.es

Botellas y Latas 087
Calle Regina 15
T 954 293 122
www.elclubdelgourmet.es

C

El Caballo 080
Calle de Antonia Díaz 7
T 954 218 127
www.elcaballo.com

Café Boheme 048
Calle de Arfe 24a
www.cafeboheme.es

Cafe Ciudad Condal 046
Alameda de Hércules 94
T 655 557 924

La Carbonería 052
Calle Levíes 18
T 954 214 460
www.levies18.com

Carmela 070
Calle Santa María la Blanca 6
T 954 540 590
Carmen Navarro 090
Calle Rosario 4
T 954 219 379
www.carmennavarro.com
Casa Anselma 070
Calle Pagés del Corro 49
Casa Balbino 096
Plaza del Cabildo 14
T 956 360 513
www.casabalbino.com
Casa Matías 048
Calle de Arfe 11
Casa Pepe Hillo 070
Calle de Adriano 24
T 954 564 145
Casa de Pilatos 036
Plaza de Pilatos 1
T 954 225 298
www.fundacionmedinaceli.org
Centro Andaluz de Arte
Contemporáneo 039
Avenida Américo Vespucio 2
T 955 037 070
www.caac.es
Cibercentro Macarena
Tres Huertas 076
Calle José Díaz
Club Sevillano de Pirágüismo 088
Paseo Marqués de Contadero
T 954 213 997
Confitería Filella 037
Avenida de la Constitución 2
T 954 224 640
www.confiteriafilella.es

Contenedor 050
Calle San Luis 50
T 954 916 333
www.contenedorcultural.com
Cortijo de Arenales 089
Autovía A-360 km35.5
Morón de la Frontera
T 955 957 048
www.cortijodearenales.com
Cruceros Torre del Oro 088
Paseo Alcalde Marqués de Contadero
T 954 561 692
www.crucerostorredeloro.com

D
Delimbo 043
Calle Pérez Galdós 1
T 955 294 188
www.delimbo.com
Despacio 091
EME Catedral Hotel
Calle Alemanes 25
T 954 560 000
www.emecatedralhotel.com

E
Enoteca Andana 085
Calle Virgen de Loreto 6
T 954 454 176
www.andanaenoteca.com
Epona 089
Hacienda Los Nietos
Autovía N-IV km519
Carmona
T 954 148 293
www.eponaspain.com

Eslava 046
Calle Eslava 3
T 954 906 568
www.espacioeslava.com
Estación de Santa Justa 078
Avenida de Kansas City
T 954 537 626
Estadio Benito Villamarín 092
Avenida Heliópolis
T 902 191 907
www.realbetisbalompie.es

F
Fundación Real Escuela Andaluza del Arte Ecuestre 096
Avenida Duque de Abrantes
Jerez de la Frontera
T 956 319 635
www.realescuela.org

G
Los Gallos 059
Plaza de Santa Cruz 11
T 954 216 981
www.tablaolosgallos.com
El Garlochi 047
Calle de los Boteros 26
Gemasolar 102
Carretera A-4 km475
Fuentes de Andalucía
La Giralda 013
Avenida de la Constitución
T 902 099 692
www.catedraldesevilla.es
Groucho 032
Calle Federico Sánchez Bedoya 20
T 657 533 471
www.grouchobar.com

H
Hijos de E Morales 070
Calle García de Vinuesa 11
T 954 221 242
Horacio Restaurante 048
Calle de Antonia Díaz 9
T 954 225 385
www.restaurantehoracio.com
Hotel Alfonso XIII 024
Calle San Fernando 2
T 954 917 000
www.luxurycollection.com/alfonsoxiii
Hotel Doña Maria 054
Calle Don Remondo 19
T 954 224 990
www.hdmaria.com

I
Infanta 048
Calle de Arfe 32-36
T 954 229 689
www.infantasevilla.es
Isadora 081
Calle Pérez Galdós 1
T 954 222 750
www.isadoratienda.blogspot.com

J
Jaylu 064
Calle López de Gomara 19
T 954 339 476
www.restaurantejaylu.com

M
La Maestranza 014
Paseo de Cristóbal Colón 12
T 954 224 577
www.realmaestranza.com

Manuel Gavira 082
Calle Gracia Fernández Palacios 3
T 954 226 703
www.manuelgavira.com
Mercadillo del Parque Alcosa 080
Avenida de Emilio Lemos
Mercado de la Calle Feria 080
Calle Feria
Mercado el Jueves 080
Calle Feria
Mercado de Triana 080
Plaza del Altozano
T 954 623 151
Metropol Parasol 044
Plaza de la Encarnación
Mezquita 101
Calle de Torrijos
Cordoba
www.mezquitadecordoba.org
Monumento a la Tolerancia 040
Paseo Alcalde Marqués de Contadero
Museo de Bellas Artes 032
Plaza del Museo 9
T 954 786 500
www.museodebellasartesdesevilla.es

N
Nuevo Gastromium 049
Calle Ramón Carande 12
T 954 625 555

O
O'Kean 080
Plaza Nueva 13
T 954 229 963
www.okeansastreria.com

P
Pabellón de Finlandia 073
Calle Marie Curie 3
www.fidas.es
Pabellón de la Navegación 072
Camino de los Descubrimientos 2
T 954 043 111
www.pabellondelanavegacion.es
Palacio Arzobispal 032
Plaza Virgen de los Reyes
Palacio de San Telmo 009
Avenida de Roma
T 955 035 500
Parque del Alamillo 088
Cortijo de Alamillo
www.parquedelalamillo.org
Parque de María Luisa 088
Avenida de María Luisa
Pedro Algaba 070
Calle de Adriano 9
T 955 091 511
Puerto Delicia 060
Muelle de las Delicias
T 955 115 656
www.puertodelicia.es
Puerto Gelves 088
Autovía Sevilla-Coria del Río km3.5
T 955 761 212
www.puertogelves.com

R
Real Alcázar 034
Patio de Banderas
T 954 502 324
www.alcazarsevilla.org

Real Club de Golf 088
Autovía Sevilla-Utrera km3.2
T 954 124 301
www.sevillagolf.com

Real Fábrica de Tabacos 009
Calle San Fernando
T 954 551 000

República Café 058
Alameda de Hércules 27
T 954 909 435
www.republicacafesevilla.blogspot.com

Robles Laredo 042
Calle de las Sierpes 90
T 954 293 232
www.casa-robles.com

S

Sala Boss 048
Calle del Betis 67
www.salaboss.es

San Ignacio de Loyola 074
Avenida de Pedro Romero
T 954 518 727

Sol y Sombra 056
Calle Castilla 147-151
T 954 333 935
www.tabernasolysombra.com

Solo Padel 088
Calle La Red Diecisiete 53
T 955 119 404
www.solopadelsevilla.es

T

El Tendido 065
Gran Meliá Colón
Calle Canalejas 1
T 954 505 599
www.gran-melia-colon.com

Tierra Nuestra 080
Calle Constancia
T 954 452 119
www.tierranuestra.es

Torre del Oro 009
Paseo de Cristóbal Colón
T 954 222 419

Torre Triana 077
Calle Juan Antonio de Vizarrón

Torres de Hércules 097
Las Marismas de Palmones
Los Barrios
Bahía de Algeciras

Tribeca 038
Calle Chaves Nogales 3
T 954 426 000
www.restaurantetribeca.com

V

Victorio & Lucchino 080
Calle de las Sierpes 86
T 954 227 951
www.victoriolucchino.com

Vinería San Telmo 068
Paseo Catalina de Ribera 4
T 954 410 600
www.vineriasantelmo.com

Z

Zelai 062
Calle de Albareda 22
T 954 229 992
www.restaurantezelai.com

HOTELS
ADDRESSES AND ROOM RATES

Hotel Adriano 016
Room rates:
double, from €60
Calle de Adriano 12
T 954 293 800
www.adrianohotel.com

Alcoba del Rey 021
Room rates:
double, from €100;
Princess Zaida, €120;
Ibn Firnas, €140;
Beatriz de Suabia, €140
Calle de Bécquer 9
T 954 915 800
www.alcobadelrey.com

Hotel Alfonso XIII 024
Room rates:
double, from €285;
Junior Suite 203, €465
Calle San Fernando 2
T 954 917 000
www.luxurycollection.com/alfonsoxiii

Almansa 11 020
Room rates:
Studio, from €180
(two-night minimum stay);
Apartment 5, from €180
Calle Almansa 11-13
T 670 343 343
www.almansa11.com

Hotel Casa 1800 026
Room rates:
double, from €150;
Junior Suite, from €240
Calle Rodrigo Caro 6
T 954 561 800
www.hotelcasa1800sevilla.com

Las Casas de la Judería 022
Room rates:
double, from €115;
Room 701, €250
Plaza de Santa María La Blanca 3
T 954 415 150
www.casasypalacios.com

Las Casas del Rey de Baeza 031
Room rates:
double, from €90;
Room 44, from €155
Calle Santiago 2
Plaza Jesús de la Redención
T 954 561 496
www.hospes.com

Corral del Rey 030
Room rates:
double, from €310;
Junior Suite 5, €420
Calle Corral del Rey 12
T 954 227 116
www.corraldelrey.com

Hotel Doña María 054
Room rates:
double, from €80
Calle Don Remondo 19
T 954 224 990
www.hdmaria.com

EME Catedral Hotel 027
Room rates:
double, from €120;
Deluxe, €350;
Deluxe Con Vistas 103, from €350;
Grand Deluxe, €1,300
Calle Alemanes 27
T 954 560 000
www.emecatedralhotel.com

Finca Cortesin 098
Room rates:
double, €450
Carretera de Casares
Casares
Marbella
www.fincacortesin.com

Hacienda de San Rafael 096
Room rates:
double, from €310
Apartado 28
Carretera N-IV km594
Las Cabezas de San Juan
T 954 227 116
www.haciendadesanrafael.com

Palacio del Bailío 100
Room rates:
double, from €160;
Deluxe Room, €610
Ramírez de las Casas Deza 10-12
Cordoba
T 957 498 993
www.hospes.com

Palacio de Villapanés 017
Room rates:
double, from €610;
Palacio Suite 202, €1,500;
Torreón Suite, €1,530
Calle Santiago 31
T 954 502 063
www.almasevilla.com

Sacristía de Santa Ana 016
Room rates:
double, €50
Alameda de Hércules 22
T 954 915 722
www.hotelsacristia.com

WALLPAPER* CITY GUIDES

Executive Editor
Rachael Moloney

Editor
Jeremy Case
Authors
Rupert Eden
Alexander Fiske-Harrison

Art Director
Loran Stosskopf
Art Editor
Eriko Shimazaki
Designer
Mayumi Hashimoto
Map Illustrator
Russell Bell

Photography Editor
Elisa Merlo
Assistant Photography Editor
Nabil Butt

Chief Sub-Editor
Nick Mee
Sub-Editor
Farah Shafiq

Editorial Assistant
Emma Harrison

Interns
Charlotte Tillieux
Romy van den Broeke

Wallpaper* Group Editor-in-Chief
Tony Chambers
Publishing Director
Gord Ray
Managing Editor
Oliver Adamson

Wallpaper* ® is a registered trademark of IPC Media Limited

First published 2009
Revised and updated 2013

All prices are correct at the time of going to press, but are subject to change.

Printed in China

PHAIDON

Phaidon Press Limited
Regent's Wharf
All Saints Street
London N1 9PA

Phaidon Press Inc
180 Varick Street
New York, NY 10014

Phaidon® is a registered trademark of Phaidon Press Limited

www.phaidon.com

A CIP Catalogue record for this book is available from the British Library.

All rights reserved.
No part of this publication may be reproduced, stored in a retrieval system or transmitted, in any form or by any means, electronic, mechanical, photocopying, recording or otherwise, without the prior permission of Phaidon Press.

© 2009 and 2013
IPC Media Limited

ISBN 978 0 7148 6608 6

PHOTOGRAPHERS

Roger Casas
Seville city view,
inside front cover
Puente del
Alamillo, pp010-011
Alameda de Hércules, p012
La Giralda, p013
La Maestranza, pp014-015
Palacio de Villapanés,
p017, pp018-019
Almansa 11, p020
Alcoba del Rey, p021
Las Casas de la
Judería, pp022-023
Hotel Alfonso XIII,
p024, p025
Hotel Casa 1800, p026
EME Catedral Hotel, p027,
pp028-029
Corral del Rey, p030
Las Casas del Rey
de Baeza, p031
Hotel Alfonso XIII, p033
Real Alcázar, pp034-035
Casa de Pilatos, p036
La Adriática, p037
Tribeca, p038
Centro Andaluz de Arte
Contemporáneo, p039
Monumento a la
Tolerancia, pp040-041
Robles Laredo, p042
Delimbo, p043
Metropol Parasol,
pp044-045
Eslava, p046
El Garlochi, p047
Nuevo Gastromium, p049
Contenedor, p050
Arte y Sabor, p051
La Carbonería, pp052-053
Hotel Doña Maria, p054
Abades Triana, p055
Sol y Sombra, pp056-057
República Café, p058
Los Gallos, p059
Puerto Delicia, p060, p061
Zelai, pp062-063
Jaylu, p064
Antique Theatro,
pp066-067
Vinería San Telmo, p068
Abantal, p069
Pabellón de
Finlandia, p073
San Ignacio de
Loyola, pp074-075
Cibercentro Macarena
Tres Huertas, p076
Torre Triana, p077
Estación de Santa
Justa, pp078-079
Isadora, p081
Manuel Gavira,
p082, p083
Arsenale, p084
Aurora Gaviño, p086
Botellas y Latas, p087
Epona, p089
Carmen Navarro, p090
Despacio, p091
Estadio Benito
Villamarín, pp092-093
Aire de Sevilla, p094, p095

Nicolás Haro
Ángel Luis Carmona, p071

Christoffer Rudquist
Lustau East India Solera
sherry, p085

**Rafael Jáuregui/age
fotostock/SuperStock**
Torres de Hércules, p097

SEVILLE
A COLOUR-CODED GUIDE TO THE HOT 'HOODS

LA MACARENA
Flamenco, tapas and nuns selling homemade delicacies – this barrio is undiluted Seville

LOS REMEDIOS
Sophisticated sports clubs and the annual flamenco fiesta are the highlights of this 'hood

LA CARTUJA
Cross the river to view contemporary architecture and art, and check out the hip clubs

EL ARENAL
Toreros thrill the fans at La Maestranza, while the riverbank offers more chilled pursuits

MARÍA LUISA
Stroll through the parkland and marvel at the cinematic spectacle of Plaza de España

TRIANA
Top tapas and a raft of nightlife options make this area a magnet for Seville's socialites

SAN VICENTE
This revitalised district has been transformed into the haunt of the city's creative set

SANTA CRUZ
The most visible remnants of Moorish Seville border this picturesque medieval quarter

For a full description of each neighbourhood, see the Introduction.
Featured venues are colour-coded, according to the district in which they are located.